COMPARING
ANIMAL TRAITS

PANTHER CHAMELEONS

COLOR-CHANGING REPTILES

REBECCA E. HIRSCH

Lerner Publications ◆ Minneapolis

Lerner Publications Company
A division of Lerner Publishing Group, Inc.
241 First Avenue North
Minneapolis, MN 55401 USA

For reading levels and more information, look up this title at www.lernerbooks.com.

Photo Acknowledgments

The images in this book are used with the permission of: © Danita Delimont/Alamy, p. 1; © Chris Mattison/Alamy, p. 4; © Nigel Pavitt/AWL Images/Getty Images, p. 5; © Chris Mattison/FLPA/Science Source, p. 6; © iStockphoto.com/fotoclick, p. 7; © Tom Cockrem/Lonely Planet Images/Getty Images, p. 8; © taboga/Shutterstock.com, p. 9 (left); © Juan Carlos MuÃ±oz/age fotostock/Getty Images, p. 9 (right); © NHPA/SuperStock, p. 10; © Leonard Lee Rue III/Science Source/Getty Images, p. 11; © Laura Westlund/Independent Picture Service, p. 12; © Philippe Psaila/Science Source, p. 13 (top); © Michael Fay/National Geographic/Getty Images, p. 13 (bottom); © Piotr Naskrecki/Minden Pictures/Getty Images, p. 14; © Martin Harvey/Photolibrary/Getty Images, p. 16; © Solvin Zankl/Visuals Unlimited, Inc., p. 17 (top); © Fotofeeling/Westend61 GmbH/Alamy, p. 17 (bottom); © Nature Picture Library/Alamy, p. 18; © Premium Stock Photography GmbH/Alamy, p. 19; © blickwinkel/Alamy, p. 20 (left); © Ed Reschke/Photolibrary/Getty Images, p. 20 (right); © Susan Heller/Moment/Getty Images, p. 21; © Sari ONeal/Shutterstock.com, p. 22; © Thomas Marent/Minden Pictures/Getty Images, p. 24; © Olimpia Martinotti/Olimpia Martinotti Photography, pp. 25, 27 © JH Pete Carmichael/The Image Bank/Getty Images, p. 26; © Universal Images Group/Getty Images, p. 27 (right); © Mirko Zanni/WaterFrame/Getty Images, p. 28; © Franco Banfi/WaterFrame/Getty Images, p. 29 (top); © Anup Shah/naturepl.com, p. 29.

Front cover: © Thomas Marent/Minden Pictures/Getty Images.
Back cover: © iStockphoto.com/CathyKeifer.

Main body text set in Calvert MT Std 12/18. Typeface provided by Monotype Typography.

Library of Congress Cataloging-in-Publication Data

Hirsch, Rebecca E.
    Panther chameleons : color-changing reptiles / Rebecca E. Hirsch.
        pages cm. — (Comparing animal traits)
    Includes bibliographical references and index.
    Audience: Ages 7–10.
    Audience: Grades K to 3.
    ISBN 978-1-4677-7978-4 (lb : alk. paper) — ISBN 978-1-4677-8270-8 (pb : alk. paper) —
ISBN 978-1-4677-8271-5 (eb pdf)
    1. Panther chameleon—Juvenile literature. I. Title.
QL666.L23H57 2015
597.95'6—dc23   2015000412

Manufactured in the United States of America
1 — BP — 7/15/15

TABLE OF CONTENTS

MEET THE PANTHER CHAMELEON

A panther chameleon walks slowly along a tree branch.
It carefully puts one foot in front of the other. Its eyes move
in different directions as it looks for insects to eat. Panther
chameleons belong to a group of animals called reptiles. Other
animal groups are insects, fish, amphibians, birds, and mammals.

A panther chameleon perches on a tree branch.

Reptiles share many characteristics. All reptiles are vertebrates—animals with backbones. Reptiles are covered with scales. Reptiles are cold-blooded. Their body temperature is controlled by their environment. In sunshine or warm weather, their bodies warm up. In cold weather, their bodies cool down. The panther chameleon shares these traits with other reptiles. It also has traits that make it unique.

CHAPTER 1

WHAT DO PANTHER CHAMELEONS LOOK LIKE?

A panther chameleon is a colorful lizard. It has a large head, bulging eyes, and a long, sticky tongue for catching insects. From the nose to the tip of the tail, male panther chameleons can be up to 22.5 inches (57 centimeters) long. They weigh an average of 2.1 ounces (60 grams). Females weigh about 0.8 ounces (23 g).

Panther chameleons can change the color of their skin. Males can be lime green, blue green, or even bright pink. They can turn dark blue or break out in red or orange stripes. Females are often light brown or green. They can change to pink or black with orange spots.

DID YOU KNOW?

Skin-color changes in panther chameleons are made by color-producing particles called pigments. When cells containing different colored pigments grow or shrink, the lizard's skin color CHANGES.

A panther chameleon's tail is as long as its body.

Panther chameleons have remarkable tails and feet. Their tails, which are as long as their bodies, can grab branches. The tails coil up when not in use. A panther chameleon's foot has three toes that are fused, or joined, on one side. They also have two fused toes on the other side of their foot. These mitten-shaped feet help the chameleon grip branches.

A panther chameleon's big eyes are covered by cone-shaped eyelids. The upper and lower eyelids are connected, leaving only a small hole to see through. Each eye moves separately, so a panther chameleon can look in two directions at once!

PANTHER CHAMELEONS VS. PARSON'S CHAMELEONS

A Parson's chameleon climbs slowly up a tree in the rain forest. Step by step, its mitten-like feet grip the branch. Parson's chameleons are bigger than panther chameleons. Parson's chameleons can grow to 28 inches (71 cm) long. Some Parson's chameleons have bumps that look like horns on their heads.

Both Parson's chameleons and panther chameleons can change the color of their skin. Female Parson's chameleons may be green, blue green, or reddish brown. Males may be green, turquoise, blue, or yellow. Parson's chameleons can also change color to brown or black. They may break out in dark bands or flecks.

Like panther chameleons, Parson's chameleons have long, sticky tongues for catching insects. They both have special, mitten-shaped feet for grasping branches and bulging eyes that can look in two different directions at once.

Parson's chameleons use their mitten-like feet to climb tree branches.

COMPARE IT!

PANTHER CHAMELEONS **VS.** **PARSON'S CHAMELEONS**

16 TO 22.5 INCHES (41 TO 57 CM)	◀ LENGTH ▶	**16 TO 28 INCHES** (41 TO 71 CM)
FUSED TOES FOR GRIPPING	◀ FEET ▶	**FUSED TOES FOR GRIPPING**

Move separately	◀ EYES ▶	Move separately
LONG AND STICKY	◀ TONGUES ▶	**LONG AND STICKY**

PANTHER CHAMELEONS VS. ALLIGATOR SNAPPING TURTLES

An alligator snapping turtle trudges through a swamp in North America. These turtles are much bigger than panther chameleons. A large alligator snapping turtle can grow to be 31 inches (79 cm) long and weigh more than 175 pounds (79 kilograms). It is one of the largest freshwater turtles in the world.

Alligator snapping turtles and panther chameleons look different. Panther chameleons often change the color of their skin. Alligator snapping turtles cannot change their skin color. They come in only one shade, a dusty brown. This drab color helps the turtle blend in with the bottoms of lakes and rivers and avoid predators.

A panther chameleon has a long, insect-zapping tongue for catching food. But an alligator snapping turtle has a small, worm-shaped projection on its short tongue. The turtle waits underwater with its mouth open wide. Curious frogs or fish are drawn to the wormlike projection on the tongue. The hungry turtle snaps its jaws closed and catches a meal.

DID YOU KNOW?
The alligator snapping turtle can stay underwater for **FIFTY MINUTES.**

CHAPTER 2

WHERE DO PANTHER CHAMELEONS LIVE?

Most chameleons live in warm places. Many species live in Africa or the island of Madagascar. A few species live in Asia and Europe. Panther chameleons dwell in the warm, moist rain forests of Madagascar.

Panther chameleons are adapted to live in trees and shrubs. They move slowly along branches, taking one step at a time. Their mitten-like feet help them balance on branches. Each foot clamps all the way around thin limbs. They can also grip branches with their tails and climb tree trunks with their sharp claws.

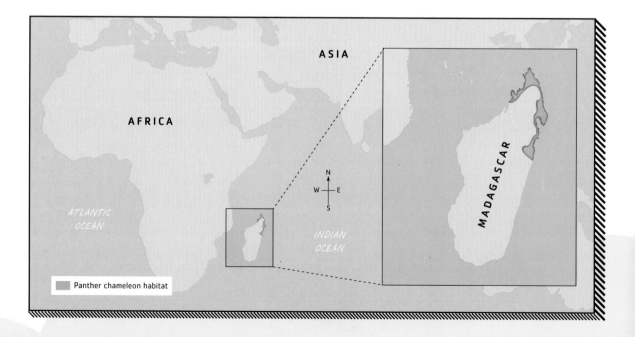

ASIA

AFRICA

N
W E
S

ATLANTIC
OCEAN

INDIAN
OCEAN

MADAGASCAR

Panther chameleon habitat

A panther chameleon's claws help it grip tree branches.

A group of panther chameleons may live close together. But each chameleon inhabits its own territory. Panther chameleons seek out trees near rivers, along roads, or in farm fields. They like open spaces where they can warm their bodies in the sun.

DID YOU KNOW? More than **150 SPECIES** of chameleons live on Earth. Almost half of the species live on the island of Madagascar.

PANTHER CHAMELEONS VS. EMERALD TREE BOAS

Emerald tree boas slither along branches in South America. With their long, green bodies, these snakes don't look like panther chameleons. But the two reptiles live in similar habitats.

Both panther chameleons and emerald tree boas inhabit rain forests. Just like panther chameleons, emerald tree boas are comfortable climbing trees. They almost never go down to the ground.

Emerald tree boas spend most of their lives in trees.

COMPARE IT!

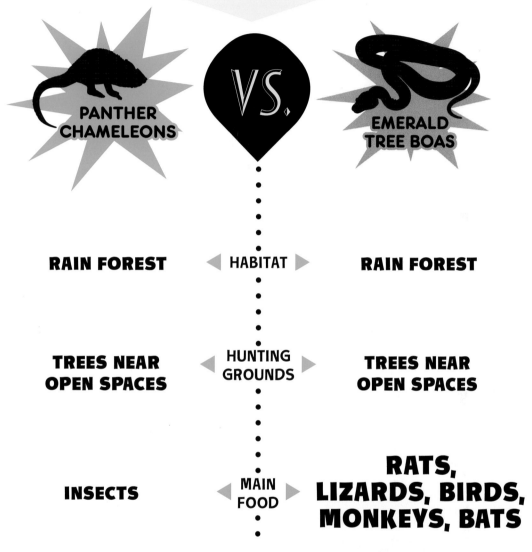

PANTHER CHAMELEONS VS. **EMERALD TREE BOAS**

PANTHER CHAMELEONS		EMERALD TREE BOAS
RAIN FOREST	◄ HABITAT ►	RAIN FOREST
TREES NEAR OPEN SPACES	◄ HUNTING GROUNDS ►	TREES NEAR OPEN SPACES
INSECTS	◄ MAIN FOOD ►	RATS, LIZARDS, BIRDS, MONKEYS, BATS

Emerald tree boas, like panther chameleons, prefer trees near open spaces. Emerald tree boas often hunt from trees next to rivers. The snake loops its thick body over a branch and waits for rats, lizards, and other prey. Its strong tail anchors the snake to the branch.

PANTHER CHAMELEONS VS. WEB-FOOTED GECKOS

Web-footed geckos scurry across the sand. These reptiles dart about in search of crickets and spiders to eat. Web-footed geckos and panther chameleons live in different habitats.

Panther chameleons inhabit rain forests where there is plenty of water. Web-footed geckos survive in the Namib Desert of southern Africa where little rain falls. But there is moisture. Morning fog rolls in from the nearby ocean. Tiny drops of water from the fog settle on the bodies of web-footed geckos. The geckos lick these droplets.

Web-footed geckos have pinkish-brown skin, webbed feet, and enormous eyes.

Panther chameleons live in trees. Web-footed geckos live on the ground. Their webbed feet help the geckos stay on top of the sandy ground in the desert. Their feet also act as shovels, helping them dig burrows beneath the sand.

A web-footed gecko digs a burrow.

DID YOU KNOW?
Web-footed geckos make **SOUNDS** to communicate, such as clicks and peeps.

CHAPTER 3

PANTHER CHAMELEONS IN ACTION

A panther chameleon perches quietly on a branch. Its eyes move in two directions at once. If it spots an insect, both eyes focus on the prey. Out shoots the chameleon's long, wet tongue. Zap! The tongue slaps against the insect and sticks tight.

Panther chameleons have long and sticky tongues that help them catch prey from a distance.

If a predator or another male chameleon enters the panther chameleon's territory, the panther chameleon opens its mouth wide. It puffs up its body with air and hisses. It is telling the intruder to back off. If the intruder doesn't leave, the chameleon leaps forward and bites with its sharp teeth.

Panther chameleons change color as a way to communicate with other panther chameleons. Colors also reflect a panther chameleon's mood. If a male panther chameleon is calm, it stays lime green or dark green. But if it spots another chameleon in its territory, it flashes stripes of red as a warning. If two males fight, both flash their warning colors. If a male doesn't want to fight, he turns dark blue or black and retreats.

DID YOU KNOW?
Male panther chameleons are always ready to **FIGHT**, but they are most aggressive during mating season.

PANTHER CHAMELEONS VS. GREEN ANOLES

A green anole scurries along a tree branch. These slender lizards search for insects in shrubs, vines, and trees in the southeastern United States. As with chameleons, green anoles can change their skin color.

Like panther chameleons, green anoles are fierce fighters. Males fight other males to defend their territory and to keep rivals away from females. When two male anoles fight, they circle each other and bob their heads. Each puffs out its dewlap, a pinkish-red flap of skin on its throat. The anoles open their mouths to show their teeth. They rush forward to bite.

When threatened by a rival, the panther chameleon (*left*) puffs up its body and hisses. The green anole (*right*) puffs out its dewlap.

Green anoles can be shades of green or brown. The lizards use the color of their skin to communicate, much as panther chameleons do. A green anole's skin color depends not only on its mood but also its temperature. Green anoles turn green in sunlight. In shade, they change to brown.

PANTHER CHAMELEONS VS. SIX-LINED RACERUNNERS

A six-lined racerunner munches on a grasshopper. Six-lined racerunners live in fields, woodlands, and sand dunes across the southeastern and midwestern United States. These sleek reptiles behave differently than panther chameleons.

Panther chameleons hunt by staying still and watching for prey. But six-lined racerunners sprint across the ground looking for insects to eat. Panther chameleons often fight other panther chameleons to protect their territory. But six-lined racerunners don't usually fight one another.

Six-lined racerunners are fast on their feet.

COMPARE IT!

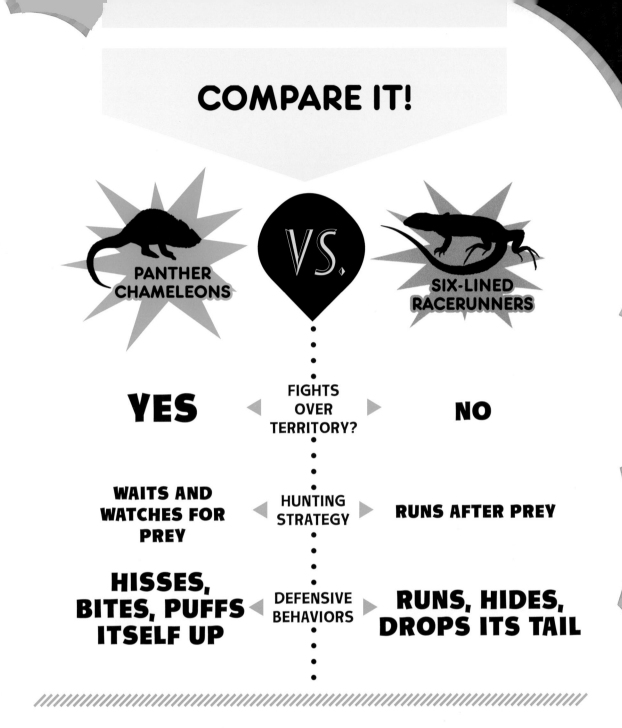

PANTHER CHAMELEONS	VS.	SIX-LINED RACERUNNERS
YES	FIGHTS OVER TERRITORY?	**NO**
WAITS AND WATCHES FOR PREY	HUNTING STRATEGY	**RUNS AFTER PREY**
HISSES, BITES, PUFFS ITSELF UP	DEFENSIVE BEHAVIORS	**RUNS, HIDES, DROPS ITS TAIL**

A panther chameleon fights back against predators. A racerunner, on the other hand, prefers to run and hide. The speedy lizard zips in a stop-and-go pattern to confuse predators. It hides in leaves, under stones, or in burrows. If the racerunner is caught, its tail breaks off. This sometimes allows the lizard to escape. A new, shorter tail will grow in its place.

CHAPTER 4
THE LIFE CYCLE OF PANTHER CHAMELEONS

The panther chameleon life cycle begins when a male and a female mate. When a male comes near a female, the female signals to him with her colors if she is ready to mate. She turns orange or pink and then changes to black with orange or pink markings. The male bobs his head and shows her his bright colors. If she likes what she sees, they will mate.

Three to six weeks after mating, the female chameleon is ready to lay her eggs. She climbs down from her tree and digs a burrow in a safe place. She lays as many as fifty eggs. She fills in the burrow and pats down the dirt. She may hide the nest by covering it with twigs and leaves. Then her job as a mother is done.

A female panther chameleon will turn orange or pink when she's ready to mate.

A baby panther chameleon hatches.

About eight months later, the young chameleons chip their way out of the eggs. Each youngster knows by instinct how to hunt and battle enemies. It has traits that were passed down from its parents. These traits, such as color-changing ability, will help it survive. In only six months, the young chameleon is ready to mate. In the wild, panther chameleons live only one or two years.

PANTHER CHAMELEONS VS. GREEN IGUANAS

A green iguana **basks** on a branch over a river. Green iguanas live in the rain forests of North America and South America. Panther chameleons and green iguanas are tree-dwelling reptiles with similar life cycles.

Female green iguanas, like female panther chameleons, climb to the ground to lay their eggs. In a safe place, the female iguana digs a nest and lays ten to thirty eggs. The green iguana mother, like the panther chameleon mother, leaves when she's finished laying eggs.

The eggs hatch two to three months later. The young iguanas, like young chameleons, use instinct to survive. Green iguanas grow up more slowly than panther chameleons. Iguanas are ready to mate in two to three years, versus six months for panther chameleons. Green iguanas can live up to eight years in the wild.

Green iguanas have longer life spans than panther chameleons.

COMPARE IT!

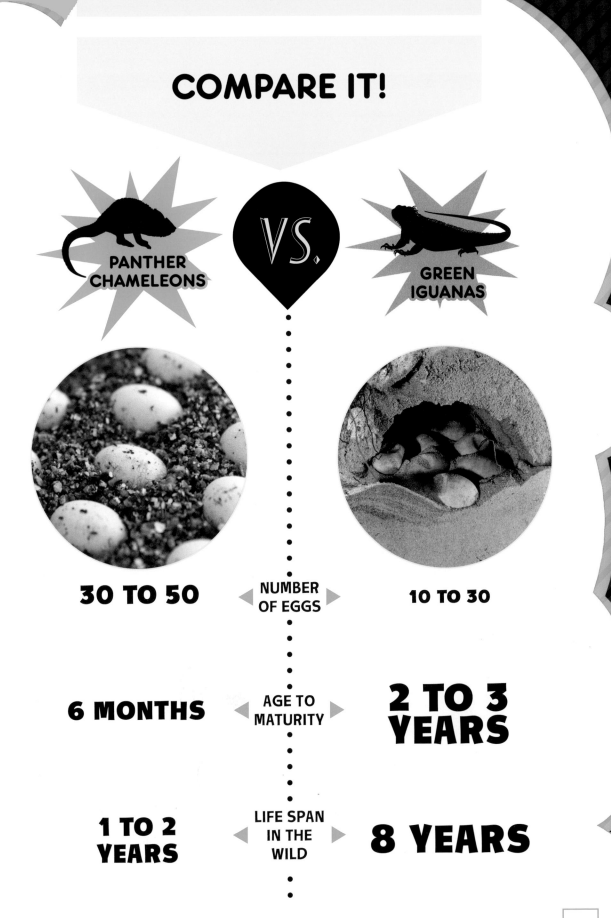

PANTHER CHAMELEONS **VS.** **GREEN IGUANAS**

PANTHER CHAMELEONS		GREEN IGUANAS
30 TO 50	NUMBER OF EGGS	10 TO 30
6 MONTHS	AGE TO MATURITY	2 TO 3 YEARS
1 TO 2 YEARS	LIFE SPAN IN THE WILD	8 YEARS

PANTHER CHAMELEONS VS. SALTWATER CROCODILES

Saltwater crocodiles glide through the water near Asia's and Australia's coasts. Saltwater crocodiles have different habitats than panther chameleons. They have different life cycles too.

A female saltwater crocodile doesn't dig a hole for her eggs, the way a panther chameleon does. A crocodile builds a mound out of grass and mud near the water. Then she lays twenty-five to ninety eggs in the mound. The mound protects the eggs from being washed away by high water.

DID YOU KNOW?
The saltwater crocodile is the largest living reptile. It can reach **23 FEET** (7 meters) long and weigh more than **2,000 POUNDS** (907 kg).

Unlike a panther chameleon, the female crocodile guards her nest. When the hatchlings begin to chirp, she digs them up. She gathers the young crocodiles in her mouth and carries them to the water. She stays with her young for several months while they learn to swim.

Saltwater crocodiles grow up much more slowly than panther chameleons. Crocodiles take ten to sixteen years to mature. They live much longer too. A panther chameleon lives only a year or two in the wild, but a saltwater crocodile can live for seventy years.

Female saltwater crocodiles carry their young to the water.

PANTHER CHAMELEON TRAIT CHART

This book introduces panther chameleons and compares them to other reptiles. What other reptiles would you like to compare?

	COLD-BLOODED	SCALES ON BODY	LAY EGGS	EYES MOVE SEPARATELY	LIVE IN TREES	CHANGE COLOR
PANTHER CHAMELEON	X	X	X	X	X	X
PARSON'S CHAMELEON	X	X	X	X	X	X
ALLIGATOR SNAPPING TURTLE	X	X	X			
EMERALD TREE BOA	X	X			X	
WEB-FOOTED GECKO	X	X	X			
GREEN ANOLE	X	X	X		X	X
SIX-LINED RACERUNNER	X	X	X			
GREEN IGUANA	X	X	X		X	
SALTWATER CROCODILE	X	X	X			

adapted: suited to living in a particular environment

basks: lies or relaxes in a warm place

burrows: holes in the ground made by animals for shelter or protection

cells: the smallest units of living things

communicate: to transmit information to other animals using sound, sight, touch, taste, or smell. Animals communicate to attract mates, warn off predators, and identify themselves.

habitats: environments where an animal naturally lives. A habitat is the place where an animal can find food, water, air, shelter, and a place to raise its young.

hatchlings: recently hatched animals

instinct: a behavior that is inherited and is automatic rather than learned

pigments: natural coloring matter in animals and plants

predators: animals that hunt, or prey on, other animals

prey: an animal that is hunted and killed by a predator for food

projection: something that sticks out

species: animals that share common features and can produce offspring

traits: features that are inherited from parents. Body size and skin color are examples of inherited traits.

LERNER

SOURCE

Expand learning beyond the printed book. Download free, complementary educational resources for this book from our website, www.lerneresource.com.

SELECTED BIBLIOGRAPHY

Badger, David. *Lizards: A Natural History of Some Uncommon Creatures— Extraordinary Chameleons, Iguanas, Geckos, & More.* Stillwater, MN: Voyageur Press, 2002.

"Chamaeleonidae." Animal Diversity Web, University of Michigan Museum of Zoology. Last modified October 31, 2003. http://animaldiversity.ummz.umich.edu /accounts/Chamaeleonidae/.

"*Furcifer pardalis.*" Animal Diversity Web, University of Michigan Museum of Zoology. Last modified February 13, 2011.

http://animaldiversity.ummz.umich.edu /accounts/Furcifer_pardalis/.

O'Shea, Mark, and Tim Halliday. *Reptiles and Amphibians.* New York: DK, 2001.

"Reptiles & Amphibians." Smithsonian National Zoological Park. Accessed November 11, 2014. http://nationalzoo.si.edu/animals /reptilesamphibians/facts/factsheets.

FURTHER INFORMATION

Bishop, Nic. *Lizards.* New York: Scholastic, 2010. Open this book for a close-up look at the world of chameleons and other lizards.

National Geographic: Chameleon Babies http://video.nationalgeographic.com /video/chameleon_babies
Watch this fascinating video to see baby chameleons hatch and begin life on their own.

National Wildlife Federation Kids: Chameleons
http://www.nwf.org/Kids/Ranger-Rick /Animals/Amphibians-and-Reptiles /Chameleons.aspx
Discover more fun facts about chameleons.

Oluonye, Mary N. *Madagascar.* Minneapolis: Lerner Publications, 2010. Read this book to learn more about the island of Madagascar and its unique wildlife.

Wildscreen Arkive: Panther Chameleon http://www.arkive.org/panther -chameleon/furcifer-pardalis
Learn more about the lives of panther chameleons with this website's photos, videos, and facts.

INDEX